Aurilla Drew

Spiced thought-food

A book for young and old containing many pen pictures in rhyme

Aurilla Drew

Spiced thought-food
A book for young and old containing many pen pictures in rhyme

ISBN/EAN: 9783337201319

Printed in Europe, USA, Canada, Australia, Japan

Cover: Foto ©Andreas Hilbeck / pixelio.de

More available books at **www.hansebooks.com**

Spiced Thought-Food,

A BOOK FOR

YOUNG AND OLD,

CONTAINING MANY

PEN PICTURES IN RHYME,

German Translations,

AND

POEMS.

PREPARED BY "AURILLA."

PUBLISHED BY
JONES & KROEGER,
WINONA, MINN.

Preface.

A word is due the reader in consideration of the seeming sudden appearance of the author.

During the past twelve years she has written with acceptance, for papers both in eastern and western cities, always however, under a *nom de plume*, and always in prose.

Many short stories have been given during this time, and "Spiced Thought" has gradually grown until friends urged its completion by publication.

It is not before the public as a sensational work, to attract by any startling history of eventful lives. It asks a welcome to your homes.

In giving it a kindly greeting may it prove a fit companion for you to linger with, and from which you may gather some thought worthy to be treasured in your memory.

M. A. DREW.

The Request.

(TRANSLATED FROM THE GERMAN.)

Bird of the green wood! come hither to me;
I have no power to soar to thee—
Yet, for thine ear I've a question rare;
'Tis a secret I keep with tender care.

O lovely, lovely bird, so bright,
I would be near thee in thy flight,
That I might hear with willing ear
The song you take to our Father dear.

Thou bright and beautiful bird of heaven;
Teach me thy strains; together then
Our clear and loudest notes we'll raise,
And give to God our highest praise.

Hours · We · All · Have · Lived.

———

Bring back, O Time, those pleasant days of old,
When youth, all bashful with its love untold,
Too modest too, to lift Hope's mystic veil,
Did blush and still love on, nor told the tale.

Bring back those precious moments, if ye will;
Sweet moments ne'er forgotten; let them thrill
Once more, my heart, that I may bow before
Thine impassioned hours enshrined there as of yore.

How gracefully doth now the fingers of old Time,
Round all my heart those sacred memories twine;
How tenderly he lifts and hangs each scene,
Then twirls and twines around each young love's
   dream.

Yes, all the flowers and fruitage of those years,
He brings to load my heart; * * * *
Why did I call them back to add a woe
To me who never more such joys shall know?

The · Strange · Star.

(WHICH APPEARED IN 1880.)

This morn at three,
I rose to gaze
Upon the new and brilliant star;
A stranger comet, some doth say,
That shines more bright, in early morn, afar.

Alone, alone,
Beside the pane
I knelt and gazed, to see its power;
Entranced I looked, and looked again,
Until, in earnest study, passed an hour.

O wondrous star!
That shines afar,
Again 'tis said, thou art the same
That led the wise men from the East
To Christ, the new born King, the King Emanuel.

O Bethlehem's star!
Art thou the same?
Then in the strangeness of thy light
And in the tumult lies the charm
Which holds me spell-bound here to-night.

What fleets before?
'Tis hard to tell,
As quickly sending forth thy flame
So bright, and of such wondrous shape,
That one must look and look to see them still again.

O star of stars!
At this lone hour
The world, it sleeps, sleeps calmly on;
It cares not for thy presence now,
And yet, for all mankind thou hast a song.

The lettered heaven,
God only reads.
He knows and calls each star by name;
Each constellation, planet, sun,
Marks a design in his great plan, as ages run.

Mysterious works
The heavens do tell,
The mystic language God reads well,
And 'twill be taught, to those who wait
To gather up the wisdom at the pearly Gate.

Thou gem of heaven!
Servant of God.
Thou hast an errand here that man
Cannot discern, or speculate
In what mysterious link you hold earth's fate.

And thou, O star,
Hast come to give
Thy light, to tell thy story unto man,
In language strange, peculiarly thine own,
'Twill be revealed; then go thy way, alone.

The·Goblet·of·Death.

FIRST VOICE.

Clay from grave in Potter's field,
Wet with tears of sorrow; sealed
With drunkard's curse, when reason reeled
In the dizzy, dizzy maniac dance of death.

SECOND VOICE.

Mingle with the black plague spot,
Fire from blazing furnace, brought
Foulest oath's to keep it hot;
Watered with the drunkard's sick, and festering breath.

THIRD VOICE.

Fill with sottish lives, the glass;
And the goblet quickly pass,
While our great prince, singeth mass
O'er the subtle, deadly mixture we have brought.

FOURTH VOICE.

Singing jubilee sonorous,
While our Master's eye is o'er us,
Guiding all the work before us,
Shouting we, responsive chorus
For the victims, to the work, which we have wrought.

CHORUS.

Wreath the cup with roses red,
To hide the viper's, venomed head.
And the asp, with poison fed; wreathing
Round, and round their slimy breath, while we,
    brightest,
Happiest, brightest, morning wed,
To phantom hopes—to joyless dead,
So we'll rake their gowling bed,
Singing, singing fiercest jubilee.

FIFTH VOICE.

Seek the manly, seek the fair,
Round them breathe thy venomed air.
Feed them with thy poison there,
Stamp on their brow, the felon's glare;
Singing, singing fiercest jubilee.

The Brook.

(TRANSLATED FROM THE GERMAN.)

O! little Brook!
As silver, bright and clear,
You always hasten to pass on, as here
Upon the bank I stand
To look and muse; I wish that I might know
From whence you came and whither on you go?

I came from out
The dark and rocky clefts;
My course is over flowery, mossy dalles;
See! on my surface;
God has to man, a finished picture given;
The reflection of the mild, serene, or stormy heaven.

As happy children,
Well do I compare,
For I dance merrily alone, scarce knowing where.
But He, who from the rocks
Called all my kin, and also bid me come,
That one must be my guide as on I run.

On·Leaving·the·Old·Church.

(FEB., 1882.)

Old church, how soon to be left,
Thoughtlessly left in silence alone;
And who from thy children heaves not
    a sigh,
As nearer, clearer, comes the cry,
Bidding us leave thy time-worn walls,
For newer, costlier, grander halls.

A sigh, —'tis not enough,
Your age is worthy more, far more.
Walls that have stood so well and long
To shield us from the cold and heat and storm,
To shield us from the storms of sin,
While we have felt secure within.

Has not our loving Lord,
Time after time given forth His breath
In pentecostal showers to save from death
Scores of sin-sick souls? These walls;
Have they not held those scenes of joy?

How many from our city,
Going backward into years far spent
Does not see himself in posture, lowly bent.
Sees himself within that sacred hour,
Warmed and illumined, by the spirit's power.

How many, many such
Have earnestly renewed their consecration,
Turning quickly from their worldly ways
Drinking deeply draughts of gladness,
As salvation turned their sadness.

If those walls could utter well,
What strange stories they could tell
Of hearts crying words like David's,
O God! renew thy spirit's power,
And cast me not away, away.
Restore to me salvation free,
Then I will surely teach thy word,
And by the sinner I'll be heard.

Such prayers have oft been raised,
While sinners too have stood amazed
At the wonders of those holy scenes,
Yes, scores of hearts been deeply touched
By hozannahs, sounding loud and clear,
Going out from hearts sincere.

I cannot leave thee now,
The dear old Church; 'tis sacred ground;
Within thy walls, my light I found; '
That light which gave to me such power
In a cold and careless, wayward hour.
I know that in my dreams your form
Will come to me to remind me well,
Of scenes whereon I love to dwell.

And now I say to thee
A sigh is not enough to make us free;
Thy children later born may laugh,
And say you now are fashionless,
And long you have been comfortless;
But I do say with heart sincere,
I'll cherish thee through every year,
And when the careless hand of fate
Begins to mar thy form so dear,
I know my heart will then be moved,
To plead thy cause, to drop a tear.

The Aunt and Niece.

CHAPTER I

The storm clouds giving forth the rain,
Released from swelling floods again
Chasing each other till chased away,
Leaving the sun to brighten the day.

In a shower of tears the story ceased,
Each heart from grief, seemed now released;
Then said a voice, in accents mild,
"Tis well, sister Kate, I'll take your child.
To my boy she'll be as a sister dear—
In sports and games shall appear
With an equal right; an equal pair;
My best affections, she shall share,
Controling each by the spirit of love,
Which comes direct from the father above."

In very good time, the little girl, Grace,
Found in that home of love, a place;
The house, with play and prattle and song,
Resounded with glee the whole day long;
Playthings spread in wild array,
In the space set apart for the children by day;

3

Tops, and block houses, and fish that were caught
By a magnet, right true. Each hour brought
Some new discovered joy, to be
Discussed. They often played dinner and tea,
On a small round stand which always stood
Ready with dishes of china and wood.

Thus weeks and months so quickly flew,
That quite two years, as by magic grew—
When early one September day,
Just as the sky was changing from gray
Into gold, and red, and purple of morn.
Another babe came to this home.

The nurse, with an experienced eye,
Saw that the toys must be laid by;
She said, "Your ma must be free to-day,
From noise of laugh and tumult of play."

Then out on the lawn, the girl and boy
Ran with the dog, in frolicsome joy.
Still, on their minds a mystery stood
When told, if they'd be quiet and good,
They soon should see the stranger sis,
And give her a pat, a hug, and a kiss.

The mother pressed to her lips the babe.
'Twas a happy event; she earnestly prayed
For patience, wisdom, and strength from above,

To help her divide her mother love
That neither one of these children three,
Should catch a glimpse of partiality.

The babe as it grew, made sunshine each hour,
To shed o'er that house its secret power.
At ten months old she had an odd way
Of laugh; she would sing and sing and play.
While Harry and Grace, on either side,
Rocked the crib in joyous pride,
Singing and laughing as moments go on,
Louder and louder grows the merry song.

The concert, was often discordant and harsh,
Till grandma rose up to exclaim, "Hush, hush,
I cannot endure,   you'll craze my brain,
Go quickly to your toys again."
The children then would scamper and run,
T'was thus every day, their concert and fun.

The time passed happily on and on,
Till two more years had come and gone.
The babe that came on that September day,
Lies hushed forever from laugh and play.
One link of the chain, tis lifted high;
God's ways are strange when his rod is nigh.

Four years from this time of affliction and grief,
Two other babes had unfolded a leaf,

Showing a page filled up with delight.
'Twas very soon read; quickly followed the night.
A grief almost too much to endure,
Yet the parents rearched for the Master's cure.
The mother said, "Though sorrow benumbs,
God now is blessing our little ones;
Forever escaped the world's rude harms,
Heaven is their home, in Christ's loving arms."

The boy and girl still played their part
With toys and games. At hours set apart
Came reading, spelling, pencil and slate,
Their work, a marvel indeed to relate.
Hours were not with weariness clad;
With loving skill, the grandma had
Made study seem an earnest play;
Hence instruction gained an easy sway.

Those hours were sunshine to that home,
Yet, to the grandma's heart would come,
Oft times a thought, to well appear
As if some lurking cloud was near.
Strong grew the thoughts within her heart,
Weighing heavily, a constant smart.

One afternoon, in August's sultry days,
At sunset when the sky was all ablaze,
In the shadow of the trees, the children run

With the dog; then in the hammock swung,
Jumping, tumbling, wild and free;
The boy was strangely given to glee.

The mother smiled as she looked on,
The father proudly kissed his son;
All seemed to be impressed as one,
That ne'er before, had they seen their boy,
So sparkling, bright; so full of joy.

But grandma, feeling the chilling cloud,
Replied, (yet speaking but half aloud.)
"It tokens no good, his mirth to-day,
Tis a rude, a very unnatural way;
His eyes are too bright, his cheeks too red,
By his nervous glee, don't be misled.
I have no doubt, but that e'er long,
Something will come to change his song."

That very day, at the midnight hour,
The mother rose to look on her boy,
Who turned so restless; tossing about;
Flashed quickly o'er her mind a thought,
Which brought again his nervous ways—
Giving the light its fullest blaze;
She read on his face the prophecy plain;
She saw it scarlet, with fever and pain,
And fear changed place with recent joy.
Placing her hand on the head of her boy

She said, "Harry dear, are you sick or in pain?"
In a voice strangely new the answer came:
"O ma! I guess I am sick; O dear!
I do feel so queer, O dear, just here."

The pain increased from that first hour,
Till the parents, taught by an unseen power
Felt the cloud of death, which hovered there.
Each day seemed ages of despair.
Yet hope doth give a parent's heart
That which oppression cannot thwart;
Sometimes to class him as a hero of renown,
Comparing well with one o'ercome
By proud ambition's highest fame,
Dashes into battle, striving for a name.

Thus passed ten days of anxious care.
To leave his bed, they would not dare.
All thought of food or rest had fled;
But hope increased, when the doctor said:
"The symptoms, soon, I think will change,
And then,— well, yes, 'twill not be strange;
(Disease oft baffles human skill);
We'll see the result, for good or ill."

Hearts of love, unskilled in art,
See not the subtle, poison dart
Of Death.   'Tis well, love's strength would fail,

Could it anticipate the doom
Which sometimes lingers near too soon
To desolate all hope and to destroy
And crush out all its life and joy.

The hours passed. In trembling dread
They waited, for the doctor's tread.
But he, knowing his errand must be
To carry only a burden of grief;
Excused himself for a later time;
The clock was well past the hour of nine
When he stood by the boy; then without speech,
He told the result to the parents each.

But grandma pressed him to say what he thought,
He simply replied, "No hope, no hope."
That day, as the light of sun went out,"
The angel of death took this beautiful boy.
Firmly grasping his silent oars,
He pushed his boat from mortal shores,
And carried him over the cold, dark river,
Into the home of the pure and blest.

When from the grave of their darling boy
They came, bereft of earthly joy.
The mother said, in anguish of heart,
"Our treasure's now, of heaven, a part.
Looking beyond, heaven will seem near,

And He who leadeth will be dear.
Going that way; ne'er turning aside,
God's holy spirit will ever abide.
Straight is the road to these treasures above,
We'll find them again, in the kingdom of love."

The husband said, "Nay! strange love is this,
That all our sweet babes, our only son,
Dear Harry, our oldest, our very first born,
Should be thus snatched from our embrace,
Leaving one, not our own, to claim his place.
Think you indeed. 'tis sent from above,
This sorrow keen, from a father of love;
Will He so chasten His children here,
Taking our every treasure away,
Leaving naught in old age, our hearts to cheer?
I'll leave this dread place, I cannot remain
Where sorrow's cup is full to the brim.
We'll visit lands where the scenes are new,
'Twill help to drive this despair from view."

"Ah, no," said the wife, "remain just here,
Where every moment sounding near,
The children's voices, as at play,
I'll hear that echo all the day.
No space in this house, but is dear to me,
And this green lawn, I know I shall see
And never forget that day on the lawn.

How they enjoyed that free wild run,
Harry driving the dog and the cart,
Grace played well the passenger part."

"This place 's to me a sacred domain;
Not one so dear shall I find again.
Go where we will on mother earth,
God's hand can reach to spread a dearth.
Can we discern with human eyes,
The brightness lighting up the skies
Beyond this cloud of dark despair?
Then let us wait God's time or care,
Why He has taken from their place,
Our children dear, leaving sweet Grace."

"We must endure this smart from the rod,
And ask for wisdom from our God,
Our minds to lead, our hearts engage
In loving duties, fill each page
Of her young life. Let nothing come
To mar the pleasure of her home,
Let our best love without alloy,
Deep stamp its marks of real joy,
And then as age draws slowly near,
Grace's sweet songs our hearts will cheer."

CHAPTER II

When many years had come and gone,
We find this Grace, a maiden grown;
The aunt, in thought, would visit again,
Those places clad in the verdure of green.
Then, quickly, like some fiery dart,
Would come a wish into her heart,
To visit once more, those days of joy,
Returning, bringing her beautiful boy;
To place him again, in his earthly home
For Grace a brother, for her a son.

Again Grace, the aunt, and grandma,
Would wander back o'er the distance far;
And Grace could almost feel the smart,
And see the drear, lone place in that heart.
'Twas then with motives tender and pure,
She would again the aunt assure:

"I am here, I am yours, daughter and child;
When you've grown old, I will provide;
You'll not be sad; you'll not be drear;
For I will then cheer you, auntie dear."

In the steady tread of grave old Time,
Years passed; by every outward sign
The parent's grief stood now afar
'Twas healed, leaving only the scar;

And a maiden fair, in years nineteen,
Reigned o'er that house, a bright sunbeam.
She who once was sweet little Grace
· Seems now holding firmly the place;
By her love and merry sweet song,
She healed the wound of that desolate home,
And made it a realm of glad delight;
She was its joy; its light, ever bright.

It was to her a Paradise that home--
And as her early years had flown,
All unperceived those tender trees
Had also grown mature with leaves
And buds and blossoms rich and rare
For Autumn's harvest. Planted there
By uncle's hand; to test the soil,
He sacrificed much gold and toil,
And these had all kept steady pace
With the unfolding years of grace.

In Springtime every bush and tree
Was clothed as far as one could see,
Superbly in a dress of white.
All who beheld the lovely sight,
Stood to admire; and many came
From far and near. Indeed the fame
Of that bright home was truly won,
When in Autumn days the juicy plum,

And grape, and golden apple rare,
Hung gracefully, as silent tempters there.

Picnics, rides, sails and walks,
Concerts, dinners, teas and talks,
Were planned within those pretty bowers
Which stood among the vines and flowers.
Youth and maidens gathered there,
So merry and free, no thought of care;
And oft the quiet moon looked down
To cheer the singers' evening song—
How many maidens all unseen,
Have watched the sacred Halloween
By Grace's chamber window pane
Rehearsing last year's charms again.

*   *   *   *   *   *   *   *   *

'Tis said no common earthly thing
Is well complete without a ring.
And thus it was these maidens dare
Conceive a plan quite cute and rare,
To form a ring of solid worth,
Made up of twenty girls and youth.
To each was given a mystic name
To suit the color, size and brain.

Of many flowers the list composed—
Grace was Bluebell; Emma, Rose;
The Pansy was for Kate a name,

And Jennie wished the very same;
But all agreed that stately trees,
Which stood the brunt of every breeze,
Would better serve for sterner hearts,
Hence "Sycamore" was cousin Mark's,
The "Mountain Ash" seemed best for Dick,
But James, was ever called "Old Nick,"
The "Giant Oak" was given to Harry—
He broke the ring—the first to marry.
Those joyous days their course spun on—
Grace too, had learned love's happy song;
And love's young dream played well its part
To lure each youth and maiden heart.
And each the secret charm obeyed,
With all his heart in love arrayed,
The world to him was one bright beam
Of sunshine clear, no mist was seen,
As merrily danced the time along,
And cherrily rings the maiden's song;
And Grace led on those feasts of joy,
Those happy hours without alloy.

*   *   *   *   *   *   *   *   *

The bridal day came, alas! too soon;
In the crowded, flower-decked room
Dressed in softest white, she stood,
Twenty birthdays for a bridal crown.
She went from this childless home so dear,

To fill some other home with cheer;
From the marriage day, through that whole year;
The time, to that young wedded pair,
Was like a dream of happiness rare.

Again old Time, with his finger of age,
Turned a leaf.　Grace saw a new page --
Word came to the aunt that November morn,
That another dear little Grace was born,
With soft light hair, and deep blue eyes,
A darling babe; of uncommon size.

Then all the friends and near of kin,
Said she was sent their love to win.
Friend vied with friend to give his share,
The mother's love was shown in prayer.
Seeing the months fly rapidly on,
There came to her heart a desire strong
To train this child in wisdom's way.
She would study, work, plan and pray,
That unto this child she might impart
Purest ideas to mould her young heart.

But with the babe's first birthday proud,
Came also unto Grace, a cloud;
Something she could not understand,
An aching head, a weary hand—
The aunty's eyes quick marked disease;

She seemed alarmed and ill at ease
When'er she looked on Grace's young face;
Often she said, "Now Grace, dear Grace,
There's a wrong, somewhere; a mystery too."
But Grace denied with smiles not a few.

One day she found the niece alone;
Seeing some signs, before unknown,
She gathered courage and said, "my dear,
You must not deny that ill draws near;
I mark the change each time I'm here.
Tell me to-day, the secret Grace,
That speaks so plainly on your face."

Emotion strong, now stirred her heart.
And quick as lightning speed the dart
To flash each feature of her face;
She had for fear, no hiding place.

With sadly measured words inclined
She said, "Dear aunt, since 'tis your mind
To judge that I a secret hold,
Which is too dark to be well told;
I think, indeed I know 'tis well,
That I to you, this secret tell.
'Tis that, I can no longer hide;
Long months ago ambition died.
And now, with a reluctant will,
I must confess, I'm strangely ill."

"It seemed so little space, since well
I closed the door, of buoyant youth,
I felt I could not tell, this truth.
To me, a few short weeks they seem,
A very short and happy dream."

"A hidden power drinks up my strength,
Perhaps disease, to some extent,
The care of Gracie is not light,
I scarcely trust her from my sight;
She's strong to play and run about,
Indeed some days I'm clear tired out."

"But listen aunt, I'll not forget
While here, in confidence we've met,
To caution, request, mildly command,
That you, when asked by any friend,
Will every question quickly repel,
I know with the Spring, I shall be well."

The words ceased.   The confession brought
To the aunt, a rush of anxious thought.
She knew disease, had long retained
Its hold, too long, had this remained
Untold.   With energy quick and sharp,
She said, "If medical science and art,
Can fathom disease, obscure and dark,
Let not one day—ah! not an hour,
Add to its grip of secret power.

With Spring, health gave no sign of cheer,
Disease worked on, stern and severe.
The aunt would often visit the niece,
And learn each added sign to trace.
And then to lift a little care,
She'd take the babe, singing an air
In cadence, softly low and sweet,
Would charm and lull her well to sleep.

Grace would lie down to think and dream,
And serious thoughts would fill her brain
When free from care. Still, in her breast,
Stood a mystery dark. She could not rest.
"My darling babe, who'll care for her,
Should sickness cast its uncertain blur,
Who then will lead her into the right,
If I fade out with canker and blight."
These were thoughts which ever seemed
To form a cloud, whene'er she dreamed.
 *   *   *   *   *   *   *   *   *
Many a time the aunt looked on,
As Grace hummed low, the cradle song.
Again and again, day after day,
She noted well, Grace's dreamy way,
And wisely guessed, that e'en a breath,
Laden with a serious hint, was death.
One day, with an indifferent air,
She called the bird; with pertence fair

She said, (lifting the bird cage door)
"Grace, come home, for a month or more.
I think you are not quite aware,
That you must now, be freed from care."

"My room below,—'twill surely serve
Your purpose well.   You 'r weak of nerve,
Deserving more than hired skill,
To nurse your weakness and your ill."

"Yes, auntie dear, if you could know
How utterly weak I am just now.
There's many duties I forsake;
I've no real pain; 'tis a steady ache;
There is no time, when I'm awake,
But that I feel a weariness great."

"Really Grace, your words now seem
Like sounds of echos, a distant dream
Ah, yes, I catch the words; 'twas mother,
She spoke to me as would no other—
Three months ago, you rode with Harry
To our gate; you would not tarry
But for a word; only a greeting.
Do you recall that hasty meeting?
Her words,—well, let this suffice;
She said, " 'Twas easy to read in your eyes,
And plainer still, disease she traced,
In the color and lines of your dear face."

But see the carriage by the gate,
Good-bye now, our tete-a-tete.
But how to reach the carriage?--Tell.
The coachman answered the question well,
By entering from the walk outside,
And taking Grace in his arms as a child,
Tenderly, as he reached the street,
Lifted her up to the cushioned seat.

At home once more, grandma will say,
"Children, you've acted in haste to-day."
" 'Tis true, it was an impulse of thought,
But haste sometimes, has wonders wrought-
I think, I never before have seen
The grass and trees more beautiful green—
Lift gently John, as you held me before,
Your arms are strong; I feel quite secure.

"Take my hat auntie dear, my veil and shawl,
Hang them on the very same hooks in the hall;
I cannot explain, you know what I mean,
These rooms, every one are all the same
As when I left—I used to look
And put in order, every nook.
If I had strength to go one flight
To mine; ah then ! I'd sleep there to-night.

"How pleasant it seems; everything here,
And aunt and grandma will be near,

Their voice, and every step I'll hear
The live-long day; 'twill well atone,
And being content, when left alone."

There is a strange, a restful feeling
Through all my soul and pulses stealing;
I need this quiet, passive rest,
Which this old home can give me best.
And yet, 'tis all uncertain. anyway,
How this harp of thousand strings will play;
I know its tones are strange to me- -
Ah! it is not as it used to be."

*   *   *   *   *   *   *   *   *

The days with common care, passed on;
Grace still remained in that old home.
A strength the same, she yet possessed;
She well enjoyed that quiet rest.
Friends came; with loving sincere air
Many prescribed their remedies rare.
These said, "visit the cool sea shore."
While others advised "a southern tour;"
But Grace, very courageous and brave
Felt 'twas a journey East she craved.

To grandma, one day, she quietly said—
"Regarding my trip, I cannot evade
One thought.   A vision of bridal array.
The time seems short since that bright day;

I cannot dispel that scene of display."--
Those words, went to the auntie's heart
Their meaning to see, only in part.

*   *   *   *   *   *   *   *   *

Hearing their plans, the doctor said,
          "The time draws near,
          I must impart
My thoughts.   A conception of the end
Which soon, must come to Grace, my friend.

          "Her thoughts now run
          O'er many a clime,—
Mark this — she must not leave your home,
Far into stranger lands to roam.

          "There is no cure.
          Then be content.
The world contains no air more pure,
Than that which floats around your door."

          "In common words,
          I now will say
That death, with its invading force,
Has changed the life-blood, in its course.

          Then came a dearth;
          Its brightness fled.
It lost its qualities of worth,
And now, must soon return to earth.

Man has no art
To deal with death,
When once his poisoned, fiery dart
Is fixed to strike a vital part."

Those words to the aunt, like a dismal song,
Darkened the brightness of that morn.
She hid them deep in her loving heart,
Still working on to stay the result.

CHAPTER III.

Working, watching, with little to cheer,
The time now came when she saw clear,
That Grace, each day, grew weaker and less.
Until 'twas a cruel task, to be dressed.

One morn, deep blue the sky o'erspread;
A few white clouds above, which sped
In haste before the gentle breeze
That also played among the leaves;
While to and fro, in balmy air
Sweetly sang the merry bird choir;
Over, under, and on the trees,
Singing merrily; flying with ease—
A jubilee of perfect praise,
Inviting man, his thanks to raise.

And Grace, still in the auntie's care,
Reclined on the lounge, while the aunt combed her
    hair.
Each seemed given to revery deep;
Grace's mind was filled up with "ifs;"
She turned them over and over again;
No one knows how they filled her brain,
Or how her thoughts went to many or few
Yet we'll guess the space o'er which they flew
Was wondrous large, a mystic realm,
Covering the space, 'twixt earth and heaven.
She carried the husband and child in thought,
And many plans, her mind then wrought.

But the auntie, thought on the doctor's words,
And within her heart anguish stirs.
His voice and prophesy rang in her ear;
She saw the result fast drawing near.
She knew that death was working his art.
And from a quick, gathering anguish of heart,
A burning tear, forced itself to the cheek,
And suddenly dropped to the face of the niece.

'Twas an electric spark, which told
The story well in language not too bold.
Strength came to Grace; in an instant of time
She raised herself to half recline.
One glance of strangest scrutiny,

As gazing far, into futurity.
Then with a calm and quiet dignity,
She asked, "What is eternity?"
Then with a quick transfer of thought,
And with seeming courage fraught—

"Here in this little niche of time,
I'll speak a truth; dear auntie, mine;
      I know your heart,
      And why 'tis riven;
      It is because
      A mother's love
      To me, you've given.

"And uncle too, has ever tried
To satisfy my youthful pride.
      His heart is full
      Of tenderness;
      I would repay
      His thoughtfulness.

"Alas! 'tis vain—I cannot stay,
Those deeds of love to well repay—
      Friends oft exchange,
      Gifts bought with gold,
      Their love and friendship,
      To unfold.

"My wealth, is counted not as gold,
Still, in my heart is wealth untold.
        This love, I'll leave.
        My only dower;
        'Tis all I have
        Within my power.

"But God, who counts each single hair,
And weighs the deeds of the just with care,
        Will at the end,
        Stretch forth His hand,
        To recompense
        With gifts that man
        Will never know,
        For God alone,
        Can these bestow.

"I'm weary now, and I must rest--
Charles is coming at noon with Grace.
        I'll sleep till then,
        Close the door and blind,
        Lest any noise
        Should here be brought,
        To take me from sleep
        To anxious thought."

Charles came at noon, with little Grace.
The mother slept on a longer space.

The house was dark; so quiet and still.
The dinner was eaten in silence and dread;
But each heart knew what the other heart said.

Next day grandma while talking with Grace,
Observed a change come o'er her face;
It spoke of death; and she quickly thought
Of husband and child; the two were brought.
An hour or more so strangely passed,
'Twas a sacred communion--the last.
Then other friends went in their turn,
Unto each she spoke a word alone.

When all had received her last message of love,
She said, "Dear friends there's a mansion above
Which my loving Saviour has promised me;
Its wonderful glories I soon shall see.
May God guide you all in the way of His love
Which leads to that glorious mansion above.
I'll watch for you there, watch till you come
And how cruel the thought that any one,
From this dear circle of friends and kin,
Should chance to be lost in the way of sin.
I wait; a moment seemeth an hour,-
Remember, I'll watch for you just by the shore
The favorite hymns that I've sung here;
Those precious words seem now to appear
As the very same which I shall choose
To sing, as I stand and wait on the shore."

A trying conflict; two spirits at war.
The friends, watching and counting each hour,
Knew well that death, with its conquering power,
Soon must vanquish that spirit of life,
And bear Grace away to that world of light.

Weeping and moaning no longer suppressed;
The pastor's prayer so well expressed
That separation, soon to come,
That sorrow loud from each heart was wrung.
Yet the day passed on, and life again
Seemed by some mystic spirit warmed.
She would speak again e'er her strength had flown,
One more message for her friends at home.

"I'm drawing near the unknown, heavenly land.
'Tis strange that I should think on earthly things,
Or wish indeed, one earthly act to plan,
Still, I've said before, there is one thought
That has been with me, and a mystery brought.
It has impressed me with its strangeness and its
        vagueness.
I cannot now to-day explain it well;
But yet the wish it brings me I can tell
When I am dead, put on my bridal dress;
In my hand, one spray of snowy blossoms press,
Then I shall be arrayed like as a bride
Going on a journey, with the Saviour by my side."

Those words now told the secret vein
Which, all along, time and again,
Had weighed upon her mind to stir
Her doubts, and cast that certain blur.

A few hours after those words from her lips
She passed from earth into her rest.
The aunt and uncle stood by the bed;
Their cherished hope again had fled.
And this the room, the very same room
From whence their own dear ones had flown.

They thought on those days; and this new grief
Comparing well—a counterpart
It seemed, an anquish the same to each heart.
The old healed sore; how the pains darted through.
'Twas all the heart that strangely stirred,
And yet its moanings, were not heard.

The uncle passed out; went alone by himself;
But the aunt stood by when others had left.
She smoothed the hair from the features mild
Just as she had for every child.
And she thought as she stood by the bed alone,
"O Grace, my child, you now have flown,
As a bird to the mountain top, flees from the storm.'

Then a loneliness, almost too much to endure
Filled her heart, as she looked on the dead–

"Can it be? Is it true?" (to herself she said)
"That one who took the place of our own,
And already gone with us the length of a score,
Should be struck by Death's hand and drop by the
 way,
Leaving us to walk on alone, to-day."

"Ah yes, it is true, and I cannot go on,
For into my heart no laugh or song
Will ever come,—no hope or cheer;
There's nothing for me but constant fear.
And far down the road to old age
'Tis lonely and dark—a shadowy page
Yet this is human life—   *   *   *   *
I must join again the care and strife,
Must rise in strength to bury the dead,
Then turn to life's work, in silence and dread.

"But wait! I catch a gleam of hope,
One ray so bright for me to note,
A promise true; our Father in heaven
Has unto her a spirit given.
'Twill visit our dreams by night and day,
And shed o'er us a glorious ray—
And all these sainted spirits dear,
Are hovering o'er and abiding so near
That we may partake of the influence sweet
Which comes from that strange and mighty unseen

'Twill help us on in our earthly dream,
And fill us with hope and courage supreme."

As on the winds, the news wide sped,
That Grace, the young mother Grace, was dead.
And soon, old friends, true and the same
As stood years before, now standing again,
In the same room, doing the same deed
Of friendship and love for hearts that bleed.

The scene is changed; from infancy to youth,
Yes, more than youth, to manhood's truth,
And all the friends of Grace's schooldays
Brought flowers the room to deck.
There was no lack of thought or skill,
To add one touch each seemed to will.
And from afar came flowers rare;
The fragrance more than filled the air.
Indeed each space held something choice,
Telling as plain as lip or voice,
How every young and school-day friend
Had tried to smooth the solemn end.
It seemed a sacred, heavenly bower,
So full of leaves and buds and flower.

Looking backward o'er the time,
'Tis but a few short months, we find,
Since Grace appeared in this same room

Beneath the marriage bell, which swung
Festooned with flower wreaths, and bands
Of Evergreen, arranged by careful hands.
Those vows, so full of youthful love
And earthly dreams; seemed blest above.

Yes, a few short months to seem
Since then; and now these friends
With soft and hesitating tread
Which suited well the gloom o'erspread,
Came in to comb the silken hair,
And every fold of dress prepare.—
How sad and reverently they stand,
To place within the marble hand
That spray of buds,— her last request
Before she went to heavenly rest. -
How beautiful in bridal robes
She's dressed for death's repose.
So calm, so mild, it well doth seem
To lay her down for heavenly dream.

A lovely face, sleeping there at ease,
In such a bower of perfumed leaves,
That when the aunt again beheld,
She almost wished that her own soul
Was then at rest within God's fold.

And silent was the room just then,
And she could look, and look again.
She stood alone; no friend was near,
That marble face seemed smiling on her tear—
"Surely! surely," the auntie said,
"Those lips are dead; so cold, so dead --
And yet they seem again to speak.—
Now let me listen, listen well—
It is her voice,—I hear it tell
Something that ever will be dear—
'Look heavenward, auntie, I am here.—
Call not this world a dreary waste
Because God many times has given
A bitter cup for you to taste.—
And if a mother's place to fill
On earth, God does not seem to will,
There's other work He has for you,—
The vineyard's large, the laborers few.
Let this desire of all, be the best,
To gather the stray ones into God's rest,
And when you faint and drop by the way,
'Twill usher in a glorious day
When loved ones from the spirit land
Will—waiting for you, stand
On that immortal shore to greet.
And from the time our spirits meet,
Your life will be one ceaseless joy,
An endless peace, without alloy.'"

WRITTEN BY GRANDMA, JAN. 1880.

Our precious one has gone,
 She could no longer stay,
Our Heavenly Father called,
 And she gently passed away.

We feel her presence with us,
 It seems she's hovering near,
To guard her little Gracie,
 And watch her smiles and tear.

She'd only just begun
 Life's real path to tread,
When she was called away
 And numbered with the dead.

We miss her more each day,
 Years will not hide our grief,
And all the world beside
 Can give us no relief.

Hark! the Father speaks,—
 He bids us all be still;
"Your darling Gracie's left you,
 It was my sovereign will."

"I order all things right,
 I calm the raging storm,

I only lent your treasure,
    And have taken her from harm."

"She's in the blessed mansions
    Prepared for her on high,
She ne'er will know a sorrow
    Or heave an anxious sigh."

My thoughts go up to heaven,
    I hear the angel choir,
I hear a sweet familiar voice
    Saying "grandma, I am here."

Oh when I leave this world,
    To Heaven may I repair,
And rest in Christ, the hiding place,
    For Gracie, she is there.

Matrimony's Dream.

Two loving souls, strong and brave,
Launched their bark upon the wave.
Along the shore and waters near
How calm, and sunshine doth appear
O'er all the heavens spread.--The scene
Came to their souls like a dream; a dream
Of enchantment, so strangely bright,
They noted not the moments' flight;-
'Twas more than a perfect day of light,
How could it ever end in night?

Thus they floated, merrily on,
Responding to enchantment's song—
When, suddenly there seemed to be
Sweeping o'er that lovely sea,
A phantom, moving on the crest,
Breathing softly tidings of unrest.

While the shadowy phantom passed,
Thoughts and doubts, came thick and fast,
The woman was, with nerve so strung,
That through her mind, suspicion run,--
Then she breathed a question low,

That her soul so yearned to know.—
"Tell me, tell me, will this sea
Always calm and sunny be?"
Soon the answer on the breeze,
Came to set her soul at ease.
"Dream on, sail on as before,
'Twas but a shadow, nothing more."

Quick she caught, those words of cheer,
Which dispelled all doubt and fear.
Sped they merrily as before,—
It was a shadow, nothing more.
But time, measured well each hour,
While they had not the will or power
To mark the swiftness of its pace,
As they went on love's pleasure chase.
They felt the gentle swelling breeze,
It pushed their bark, with graceful ease
Over waves, far out from shore;
And the siren's song was,—"evermore."

Thus they sailed and sailed away,
Dreaming of life, as a perfect day,—
Till,—in the far horizon came
A form!—"This the phantom again?"
"No, no, 'tis the tempest's dark cloud,
Muttered the thunder, half aloud"—
Then, as if by magical might,

The cloud spread a darkness, like night;
While the thunder's voice increased,
The enchanting song of the "siren," ceased.

Quick the flying sails were furled,
Quick the anchor, out was hurled,--
Danger seemed to linger near;
The woman was convulsed with fear,
She felt this darkness, something more
Than treacherous winds had told before,
With outstretched hands, on bended knee,
And eyes, far looking o'er the sea,
She cried for them again to hear
Her supplicating prayer of fear.

Spake the thunder, loud and long,
Lightning, marked the tempest's frown
But heeded not, the winds her cry,
And helpless sank she down to die.

E'er long the tempest spent its force,
Leaving its bark to its onward course.
Alone, the husband walked the deck,
The wife, could not emotion check;
With soft and cautious words, she said:
(Hanging her dark and graceful head,)
"Three months, since we sailed away,
And now, 'tis but the month of May.

Tell me, why was it whispered to me
That storms n'er came, on this bright sea?"

Then the husband spake and said,
"Enchantment long your soul has fed;
Looking onward, o'er this sea
The course seems clear for you and me -
If comes a storm like this in May,
What must it be on a summer day?
Prepare yourself and take good heed,
Strength, courage, patience, you will need,
✱ Enchantment's span no more will run,
Her magic spell, is now undone."

"At ease no longer, you can sail,
Reality, has lifted, now, the veil,
That you may well a truth discern
A truth which stands severe and stern.
Nature's laws are quite unmixed
With human powers, so fixed
That storms must sometimes come, to show
God's power and presence here below.
Thousands are daily launching out,
Filled with sweet, delusive, hope,
The God of pleasure has so willed,
They drift away, with oars unskilled:
All are expecting endless day,
And thus deluded, drift away."

"In the distance o'er this sea,
Is our island home to be;
Sailing onward, but a few days more,
We will reach that stranger shore.
Reality stands waiting there,
She'll give to us our stock of care;
Experience too, will also teach,
All the arts within her reach.
Casting from our hearts all fear,
Let's end this chapter with a cheer."

Reality.

The chapter ended with a cheer,
Sounding o'er the waters clear.
Soon, standing on that stranger shore,
They opened wide, their new home door.

Few the moons that numbered well
The months that wife would blush to tell,
For time, in passing gave to her
That which left upon her mind a blur.
She had within that stranger home,
Found many nooks of ill and wrong.
And yet, the husband was her joy,
Her dream of love, without alloy.

Months passed, dim grew her dream,
Dull and distasteful each new scene;
In selfishness she sought to fill—
To bend the husband to her will.
"'Tis plain as day," she would declare,
The wrong which he thought thin as air;
And oft she would in accents low,
And in measured sentence slow,
Rehearse the house-maid's saucy air,
How carelessly she swept the stair.

Again she would in angry tones
Convey to her most patient spouse
A story; well made up of lies·—
'Twas all wrong within her eyes.
One day it would be something less,
Another day she could not guess
Why, the busy lady, Mrs. Teech,
Should be so very plain of speech;
"I think, 'tis time to say, my dear,
Her words sound harshly on my ear,
From this great house, pray let us go,
'Tis all confusion, noise and show:
The doctor said,—(and this you know)
My nerves were weak. Pray let us go."

Sometimes, the husband could but laugh,
Again, be filled with pride and wrath.
Willing to show his loving care,
And to continue a loving pair,
Six times, patiently he followered her,
To find a home, without some blur,
Day by day, working to undo
The tangles, that were not a few.

One eve, he sat alone to muse;
"Alone," he said, "nothing to confuse;
This world is cold, I feel the chill;
I never dreamed of such ill will—

8

How strange now doth it appear,
That searching, searching far and near,
One cannot find a pleasant spot
In flat, hotel, or humble cot,
But soon a thousand ills do grow,
And my wife, Kate, doth temper show."

"I ne'er before had such ill will,
Something each day; enough to fill
My soul with wrath and discontent,
So full indeed, it must give vent.
But wait! I'll watch the waters now,
See for myself what makes my frau
So given to discontent, and show
Such strange unrest, that I must go
Here and there, wandering about,
Daring not to express a doubt
As to whether this wrong with her,
Sometimes doth lie, to make this blur."

"How can I trudge again behind
My trunks and worldly goods to find.
But wait! ha! ha!! a thought has come,
'Tis more than strange how thoughts do run,
This is for me a lucky day;
Yes, thoughts run queerly any way—
Now I must early fix the date

When I'll begin to urge my Kate
To try her best at household work;
I think this move will change my luck."

"Lucky indeed; I see 'tis clear,
The time draws very, very near
When one must seek another door;
Ha! ha!! why have I not before
Received this truth -yet, how can I
My courage and my wits apply
To softly break this news to Kate--
I'll hire the house, at any rate."

"This very week, she'll hear the news,
I fear—I'm sure, she will refuse;
She likes quite well to be at ease;
This plan for her will never please."

But we will guess the chapter now,
That hides that scene of lowering brow.
Let's cut it short, the time and verse,
I dare not now the scene rehearse.
*   *   *   *   *   *   *   *   *
Three months have passed.   Let's view this pair
As they whirl round with troubled air
To sweep, to cook, to dust, to wash
Alas! the husband says " 'Tis bosh!
This household care, for every day

Some plaguy grief comes in my way.
Sore fingers wrapped in butter, flour—
A finger counted every hour;
The bread is heavy, meat is tough—
Heaven help; this is indeed too rough."

"My nerves, once strong, are now unstrung
'Tis more than strange; what can be done?
It's well my mind, I have not lost;
I'll just sell out at any cost.
Why is it thus?   Why should I be
So tossed about on life's great sea
While others seem to sail at ease,
Touched only by a gentle breeze?"

Yes, sell out—good luck and cheer,
A place is offered now, quite near,
To which we can at once repair;
Heaven knows, and will my trouble share—
To-morrow then, I will begin--
'Tis really, quite a pleasant thing
To plan; but then comes stern reality-
Indeed, this life is all uncertainty."

Alone.

Alone to-night, alone.   Indeed 'tis well
In this lone hour, my thoughts to scan.   'Tis well
To breathe them, speak them, speak them quite aloud.
This pent up wrong and grief must speak—but stay!
The breezes playing, laughing at my window near—
     Can I trust them,
         If they hear?

Yes, I can trust them; trust them ever well.
Soon they'll know, the story I will tell.
Methinks 'twill change their wild and laughing play
Into a serious, quiet, sadder way.—
I must not think and think; it is not best.
     I'll speak this grief,
         Then I will rest.

The hosts of heaven are bending to look down,
Bending low, to hear these words of wrong.
Silent listeners, weighing every word—
But not to take away the choicest part,
     Robbing them of truth—
         O that poor heart.

A few hours since, I sat to read a page
From life.   It was a cold, deceitful phase,
No! I did not read, but I engaged
To listen, while another read the storied snare.
Only a page or two, but 'twas enough;
        When but half read,
                I heard enough.

And then, I felt that I must seek for her
The traitor, who had made her life a blur.
She is indeed alone; severed from all kin.
She is bereft of every earthly love,
And all this world to her seems dark and drear
        She is a lonely
                Wanderer here.

She feels this world contains no friend sincere,
Which to the eye, did once so bright appear—
Ah yes, 'tis strange, 'tis strange, that playing word
When seeming friend meets friend in confidence,
Or e'en a look, or hint of caution given
        Without some sting,
                To leave its pain within.

Too oft, within the anxious giver's heart
It leaves its sting—is that what smarts my heart
And bids me now to ask, if I can trust—

Only the breeze, that still doth linger near?
Ah yes, my heart, it bids me ask in fear
   Is there no truth
     No friend sincere?

But as I ask; before the words are done,
I dare not utter them, as they would come.
I dare not speak the question I would tell,
For there is truth on earth, I know it well.
To say that all is false, I would not dare,
   For God is truth,
     And He is everywhere.

Helpless and in despair she sought his aid.
In agony, she cried aloud and not in vain.
Boldly now, must she His praise proclaim.
He saw her human hate; her stern disdain.
He knows what certainly must be her fate,
   If now from her,
     His presence he would take.

Ah no! I will not say that she's alone –
I will not feel, that truth from earth has flown,
For God is there, He will avenge her wrong
And said the Saviour, loving, tender, true,
"Unto all who seek me, I'll come very near,"
   Then this world
     Will not seem drear.

Drear! no.   If one feels the Saviour's power
His heart is filled with truth; and every hour
He will rejoice, that in God's boundless love,
This earth will wear a livery of peace.
Then giving unto God, our meditations pure,
      He will our secrets
         Keep secure.

Gold.

When God first gave to man his wondrous birth,
He also hid beneath the bosom of the earth
That, which through all ages of the world
Would claim man's love; his common interests
    hold—
As by a touch, His mighty fingers pressed
This wealth of gold, into its hiding place.
And when, as man with skilful hands made bare
This secret, hidden treasure of the earth,
'Twas found a useless toy, so filled with dross.

But God far back in a forgotten day,
Gave also unto man a secret way
To purge this dross from out the better part.
This wealth of gold—
It must be cleansed and purified for dower,
By the God-given wisdom of the Refiner's power.

Into his heated furnace it is cast,
To leave behind all black and filthy dross,
Twice, thrice 'tis given the boiling heat,
Ere it comes out fine, pure, complete.

9

And thus analogous is human life;
A secret mine of intellectual wealth
Is deeply buried in each human heart—
A mystery to man, who dwells within this world
Of sin and cold deceit, made dark.   *   *   *   *

There is a purer, brighter world than this,
But man can never, never find a place
Within that higher world of perfect bliss,
Till the daylight of God's power is seen.

So long as any man lies buried here,
Beneath a crust of ignorance and sin,
He will not feel the pure and glorious sunlight
Of God's brighter world within.   *   *   *   *

And God's high wisdom well conceived a plan
Mysteriously set forth, and given to sinful man.
This plan so great, it stretched from age to age;
It lifted man from gloom- to try his worth,
And purge from out his nature all its dross.

Of all the saints who dwell in heaven above,
There is not one who was not, while on earth,
Plunged into the furnace of temptation's fire;
Twice, thrice have stood the boiling heat,
To come out cleansed from dross; pure, complete.

Let man not say, or try to argue well,
(For 'tis a weak and vain untruth to tell)
That all wise God will finally accept
A soul dripping with the chilly damp of earth,
All crusted o'er with doubts and blackened sin
Indeed! How could he thus so mar the brightness
Of His purified and heavenly courts within?

Ah no, he could not use such impure souls,
No more than man can use God's gift of gold—
Until, at any cost, it's freed from dross.

The Madman.

Pealing from rock to rock,
Echoes the thunder's shock,—
Earth and sky seem to rock,
    Earth and sky.

Where the storm wildest roars,
Where the winds shrieking hoarse,—
Rushing mad in their course,
    There am I.

Here the dry blistered earth
Drinks the showers at their birth.
Ha! ha! what mirth, what mirth
    This for me.

Winds shireking, sighing,
Storm king defying,
Here am I dying,
    In my mad glee.

Raving mad though I be,
Mad winds I call on thee.
Yes, ye can pity me,
    Says thy deep moan.

Wandering wild winds with thee,—
Mad! Yes, my maddest glee
Breaks from despair in me,
 For I'm alone.

Lightning stay! stay thy light,—
Each flash of thine so bright,
Recalls the cankering blight,
 In my poor heart.

Like this that night I met,
Her whom I'll ne'er forget;
I keep her image yet.
 We ne'er shall part.

Once, ye flashed wild as now,
On this same mountain brow—
Storm spirit, then, oh! how
 Black were ye; when

Sobbing upon the gale,
Shrieking adown the vale,
Thy mournful death-like wail,
 Sounded then.

Hark ye! that piercing cry!
And the tempestuous sky
Echoes it back; but why
 Our secret keep.

Why shall I tell the tale?
Hear it now on the gale.
Sob it winds in thy wail,
    I cannot weep.

There she in terror clung,
O'er that dark chasm hung
Calling —ah! human tongue
    Cannot tell.

How on that night my ear
Caught that wild scream of fear—
How, too, I saved her here,
    I cannot tell.

Lightning, stay! stay thy light,
Each flash of thine so bright
Brings back that awful sight–
    Oh! my poor heart.

Scorching my eyeballs be —
Storm clouds, come weep with me
Send thy wet tears to me—
    Sorrow has died.

Hot tears that would have flowed,
Since that night we two stood
In this same gloomy wood,
    Side by side.

Stern clouds; weep for me.
Come thou! each tear that ye
Shed for her, ye shall be--
    Ye shall be blest.

Hist! hear that voice again.
Think ye it gives me pain?
Hist! hush! I tell ye then
    She bids me come.

Where the storm blackened height,
Stands in majestic might-
That's why I'm here to-night,
    She bids me come.

She tore my heart from me—
That's why I'm mad with glee,
I am happy; so is she.
    Though she is gone.

Yet she'll be here to-night;
Tempest rage in your might,
What if my mind's a blight?
    For I'm alone.   S. H. L.

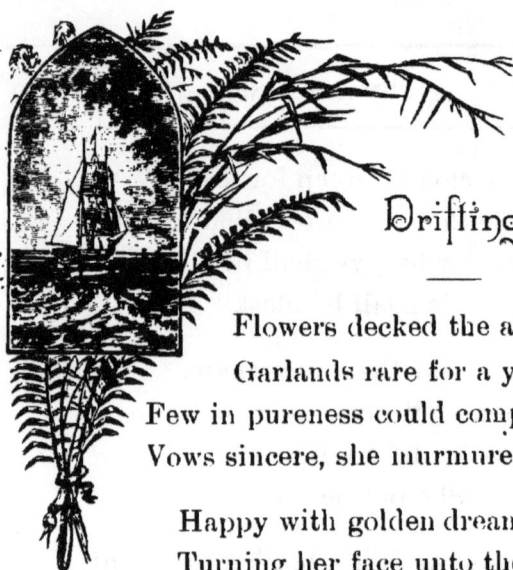

Drifting.

Flowers decked the altar's side;
  Garlands rare for a youthful bride.
Few in pureness could compare,
Vows sincere, she murmured there.

  Happy with golden dreams was she,
    Turning her face unto the sea,
The world's treacherous, heaving sea,
Her hearts it sang a jubilee.

  Long ago by the hand of fate,
    Was the husband's love turned to hate
Hate for the careless, drifting bark,
That floated at ease from virtue apart.

  Floating and feasting, enough, enough,
    Deeply he drank from Revel's cup;
Far o'er the sea, dreaming away,
Years of youth unto manhood's day.

  Tempests turned his fragile bark;
    Waves and sky; all was dark--
As summer breezes drive the leaf,
So whirled his bark without relief.

Trembling, cursing, mad with fear—
How could he welcome death so near?
Moments seemed a mighty age,
His thoughts flew o'er it; dark was the page.

Burdens of sin, hard to endure,
Filled his soul,—a soul impure.
But see! now on the angry wave
Comes a ship, to cheer and aid.

A stately ship; with holy aim
The captain sought this soul to gain.
Strong those hearts; 'twas a life to save.
God has always a work for the brave.

The captain quickly gave commands
To sailors true; whose steady hands
Flung out the rope; pulling him in,
Bearing him up to the staunch ship "Quinn."

Gazing o'er the ship's deck,
As one would from a dream awake;
Seeing the captain drawing near,
He turned to him for aid and cheer.

The captain hurriedly advanced;
Pity from his dark eyes glanced;
Strong in his heart burned his love for youth,
It forced him to speak these words of truth.

10

Young man I cheerfully welcome you here,
　Many a day I've watched your career,
Drinking your draughts from pleasure's cup
Pleasure! no, anguish at every sup.

Warnings, pleadings, again and again
　You've cast aside in scorn and disdain,
Until that cup, its poisoned dregs,
Have given to you the keenest pain.

See! look at my compass here,
　It tells me always where to steer.
Storms on this dark and treacherous sea —
They never harm or trouble me.

Dealing death to a careless crew,
　Lightly they pass o'er a pilot true;
Watching these points while sailing along,
We spend no time in jest or song.

If out on this sea one launches his bark
　Having no guide, no compass, no chart,
He'll find that the winds will carry him sure,
Into waves, on to rocks, hard to endure.

Cast now your love for pleasure away—
　Look at those rocks; you dashed on to-day;
Think not my words are meant for ill—
'Tis death! this playing and drifting at will.

Many a careless, wayward youth,
Dances and drifts away from truth,
Thinking never, of that harbor,
Where all will rest from care and labor.

Come now, my friend, abide with me,
Soon you'll learn to sail on this sea;
Learn the secret of compass and chart,
Pure, and holy is this art.

Working on, with a heart sincere,
Earnestly working, laughing at fear,
I'll promise you this—in half the days
You've given to pleasure's sinful ways.

Coming again to these same rocks,
You'll save many other tempest-tossed barks,
And from you, they must learn the story anew,
What I, on this deck now promise you.

* * * * * * * * *

The words ceased, their sounds died out;
Silent, fear held its sway on deck.
The man could not well hide or check
Emotions strong. He seemed in doubt.
Then sudden gleamed his eyes with hope,
His face changing from despair to joy
And light of love—then as if fearing
To lose one breath of time or thought,
He spoke these words of gratitude.

"Yes, my friend, your words to me
Are as sunshine after a storm;
I'm weary of drifting on this sea;
I'll stay by you; I'm sick and forlorn.
My days of youth and early manhood,
Are days of regret, I cannot recall;
They being to me now no story of good;
Your kindness is great, I'll sail along,
And learn from you that mighty art
Which gives control through dreary storm
Oh, give me of your skill, a part,
'Twill change the tone of my poor heart
Wait, let me turn the leaves of time,
Carefully turning, till I find
All the pages, ———, spotless, pure,
Ah, then, must begin—this soul cure."

"And I'll record on each pure page
Every good and honest deed
Done from motives noble, true.
Names of souls must be written there—
Souls! They are drifting everywhere;
I know too well, who are drifting away,
Thousands going by day and by day—
Surely, friend, on each pure page,
There must be no inch of space left."
*　*　*　*　*　*　*　*　*
This is the groom who stood by the bride,

Proudly waiting by the altar's side,
Speaking in accents firm and clear,
His vows of love and truth sincere.

He took his bride to his ship by the sea;
They sailed away with the gallant crew,
Sailing o'er the troubled wave,
Many a drifting bark to save.

Blest was the voyage to the bride and groom,
And when the ship again returned,
Those pages pure were filled, each space,
And peacefully, happy and full of trust
Were those two hearts as they stepped on shore,
For they felt that the Master on high knew all;
And would write in His book—the result.

In · Memory · of · May · Staples.

She was our light,
Our May so bright,
    With golden hair,
    And face so fair.
She played and chattered, chattered
    and played.
The gay dressed dolls, and painted
    toys,
The whole day long, were her baby
    joys.

Listen! she sings!
Clearly it rings.
    "Safely through
    Another week,
God has brought us on our way; —
Her every look, as she sweetly sung,
Was likeness to one from the angel throng.

How wise her sayings,
In all her playings,
    Few were the tears
    For her infant years.
All the day through wherever I go,

Her voice in my ear its echo does ring,
Softly singing that evening hymn.

When tired of play,
She had a cute way
  Of calling "mamma
  'Tis you, I want you."
Then ma, ever watchful, tender and true
Would lovingly grant little May's request,
Pressing her gently to her breast.

May seemed content
In those arms of care ---
  Indeed 'twas a picture
  Of beauty rare —
O May! was ever a child so dear?
Never indeed was a child more dear
Than our sweet, darling sweet May.

One morn in June,
Darkness came down
  To shadow the light
  Of our dear home.
The clatter ceased, her voice was low--
"I's tum mamma dear, I's tum to you
I's sick, I tant play; O dear, I want you."

A day, and more
Had quickly passed,

When sickness came
Of dangerous cast.
A sudden shock to nerve and brain,
The pulse run high; no sleep, no rest,
Her head layed lower than mamma's breast.

The father said,
"She's strangely ill,
And if it be
Just as I see,
She'll leave us soon for the heavenly way.
The symptoms now, hint strong of death,
A brain disease with heated breath.

"The remedies
I will apply;
Our duty's done
When on these we rely.
The fever hot,—'tis near high tide,
Her darling head must be cooled to-day,
These curls must be cut without delay."

That mother brave,
Her child to save
Cut every curl,
One by one.
With voice of grief she slowly said,
"In many day of months and years

I've combed these curls every morn,
Over my fingers one by one.

To-day—in this box
They now shall be
    Placed side by side,
    A treasure for me—
Then,--if May should join the angel choir.
I can still every day take her golden hair
And brush it over my fingers with care."

After her golden
Head was shorn,
    New symptoms came on,
    Till reason fled.
These were the very last words she said,
Holding a basket of odds and ends,
Candies and toys from neighbor friends:

"Here, ma, take this,
'Tis candy for you,
    And here's a piece
    For papa, too.
And a great big piece for Harry dear,
And two more pieces for pa and you—
I'se tired now and sleepy too."

With these words said
They layed her down,

And pain was shown,
The sign was a frown;
Then sudden delirium held its sway
Till overcome by the force of sleep,
Which grew into a mystery deep.

Many would watch
Our sleeping May,
But tne mother said
"Nay! nay! O nay!
Let no hand save that of love be here
When she wakes—still, should she sleep on
Never to wake, let no heart but the heart
Of love be here the care to take."

How strange that sleep,
Mysterious, deep.
The powers on high
Love's faith will try.
And just as the day its work had done,
Its work of death or life begun,
Fading away, taking the day.

So faded the light,
Once merry and bright—
There was no doubt
When the light went out,
That God did lead her safely home
Into His angel choir; and Christ
In His arms of love, will shield her there.

We're Growing Old.

Once life's summer tinted sky
  Glowed o'er us in youth's hopeful day.
But hopes have fled; life's summer's gone
  That once bright sky, is cold and gray.

Autumn winds are blowing now,
  And the trees are leafless—bare
Stand like spectres! while their moan
  Stikes a chill upon the air.

Hearts like ours would expel--
  All but the brighter side of life;
Hearts young as ours, hated well,
  With less than ours of worldly strife.

Hearts young as ours, have sought in love
  Extatic dreams—a talisman,
Their blooming hopes been blighted too
  With less of years than ours have known.

So soon our hearts are growing old;
  What shall our hopes be when the knell,
Of death, doth sweep across the soul?
  Ask of the future; it shall tell.

Where is Jesus?

GERMAN TRANSLATION.

O! Jesus, Saviour, do not hide;
Be to me again my guide.
Hast thou hidden? tell me where—
I would find thee, find thee there.

I have anguish, I have pain
For all my sins and thoughts so vain—
O! Jesus, Saviour; day and night—
I will seek and find thy light.

Now I'll call; I'll have no fear;
Tell me, tell me, is He near?
So long I've been astray from Him,
Much my heart hath turned to sin.

He can drive away my sorrow;
He can ease the pains I borrow;
Can create within my heart
A spring of joy to heal this smart.

Therefore I'll not cease to call;
Cast on Him my troubles all,
He will then my joys restore;
I will seek Him more and more.

In Memory of Hattie Frances Tourtellotte.

Nine years ago to-day
You came, to cheer our way;
To take the place of "Rosebud,"
Our darling twelve months
    "Rosebud."
Your first birthday—I never can for-
    get;
'Twas on that morn, we named you
    little "Pet."

Yes, I recall that hour;
How every gay-dressed flower
To me, looked wondrous fair;
Their perfume filled the air.
I said, "Of every flower that has
    bloomed for me yet.
I have found not one so sweet, as our
    little "Pet."

Too oft the years roll by,
Too oft, for you and I—
Come here my child! come here
I must always, have you near.
Your winning ways would grace a fairy bower,
And your sweet young heart is ripening, every hour.

This birthday; you shall be
Dressed anew; and see!
These lovely flowers were sent
As friendship's offering lent.
I'll twine a few together, for your breast,
And then, I'll make a nosegay for every little guest.

* * * * * * * * *

Six months have passed away,
Since on that bright birthday,
The mother with rare pride
Sat by her darling's side
Caressing her. How full of joy—how proud.
The day was bright. The sky sent out no cloud.

But now the winter chill,
Has brought a serious ill
To that sweet, lovely flower;
She has no will or power
To run or play; her eyes grow dull—and yet,
That mother faithfully has watched her "Pet."

"We must not linger here,"
The parents said, "Though clear
The sky; this icy breath
Of winter, may bring death."
In haste they took this bright half open flower,
Where orange groves lend perfume to each bower.

How quick her winning ways,
And natural ease and grace
Stole into stranger's heart,
Stole in, to take a part.
She found new pleasures in that southern air,
She found new charms and friendships everywhere.

But soon, a subtile ill
Appeared. An ill
Which broke the happy charm
And caused alarm.
The doctor came. He said, "Away with fears!
A simple freak it is, of youthful years."

The day passed to night,
When the sun exchanged its light
For the quiet moon, which kept
A sad and silent watch. * * *
Again the sun in all its glory bright
Arose. Fast grew the hours till noonday light.

The child raised up its head,
And with usual brightness said,
"Water, mamma—water,
Quickly! Give me water!"
One sip—then throwing back her head, was gone!
Yes, as a flash! was dead! was gone!

"Speak! speak! my child!
O God! I shall go wild!
Dead! dead? it cannot be—
Look! look and see
If she has now no pulse or breath--
O no! It cannot be the sleep of death!

"O! what a cruel blow
This sudden wave of woe—
Death aimed his fiery dart
Straight to the heart.
How can we live?   Ah! no! she is not dead—
Something whispers now, she is not dead.

"See! see! she sleeps—
How beautiful in sleep—
And yet,—she lives.
What comfort to me gives
This thought.   That now before the Father's throne
She lives!   Has entered into Life."

Free from this worldly strife,
Into that glorious life
Was by the angels borne
To that celestial home—
In that bright home beyond, give me a place,
I'll see its wonders, and my dear children's face.

"Be still, sad heart, be still.
This discipline is keen—
And I must draw more close,
More close to Him.

Be still mine heart, be still,
For in thy sorrow's night
I must bend low, bend low
And taste the cup God gives.

If from a bleeding heart
Comes pain,
My God can heal, can heal
And make it whole again."

To · the · Graduate.

TO A—— E——, 1875.

'Tis true, thy school-girl days have been
To thee a bright and joyous dream.
Thy school-girl friendships have been true,
Their tenderness and warmth ne'er knew
The influence of a soil, which gives
A force to flattery and deceit, and lives
To show unnatural coloring of art.
These friendships—hide them in thy heart
As treasures rare, ne'er soiled by tears.
Then, far away in future years
There'll come a time of doubt and fears,
When you will take those hidden treasures,
Resurrecting all their pleasures.
Time has colored every scene;
Autumn tinted now the dream,
Which gently soothes your soul to rest,
And bids your longing heart to say
These the purest, brightest, best.

The · Rich · Prince.

TRANSLATED FROM THE GERMAN, OCT., 1874.

"My Lord!" Thus spake the prince of Saxony,
  "Is not my land and his, a rich domain?
Within his mountain depths, in shaft and pit,
  The silver lies in many a shining vein.

"And see! my acres broad with plenty teem;
  Behold the waving grain; the graceful vine;
The smiling vales bestow the golden corn,
  The sloping sunny hills, the precious wine."

" 'Tis true," Lord Ludwig then to Baiern spake,
  "Thine has great cities; Convents rich has thine;
My brain cannot conceive a land like yours,
  Within the limits of our noble Rhine."

"For, did not Eberharb, the 'Broad Axe'
  Say to Wirtenburg's loved liege and lord,
'My land hath cities small, though neath its hills,
  The shining silver lies a secret hoard.' "

"And yet, methinks a greater treasure lies
  Within your smiling vales, of greater worth,
And I shall boldly choose between the two;
  Be mine the green warm breast of mother earth."

Our · Life.

Are we created here to dwell on earth,
To dream our life away in idle mirth?
Ah no, such dreams will vanish like a mist,
Before the just and holy judgment of
                              Another world.

Alas, for those who dare to dream away
A life of thoughtless ease, God's work undone,
For at the close the soul is left forlorn,
Without a passport, to that land of perfect
                              Rest beyond.

God brings man into life; marks well his birth,
And as the plant and each bright tinted flower
With its own family is classed—so we,
Receive our varied natures from the
                              Parent stock.

'Tis true, in childhood's hour we play with dreams,
And all our play seems real as the sun,
Our light and joy from face of parents beam,
While at their knee, we early learn to lisp,
                              "Thy will be done."

Then come the joyous, happy days of youth,
Thoughtless hours so filled with visions bright,
When life's one glow of dreams and pleasures rare—
Fairy castles, floating high—'Tis sunshine,
                    Everywhere.

A voice, we seem to hear, who's whispered theme
Bids us to enter and enjoy those castle halls,
For each contain some brilliant, happy dream,
Which we will never, never dream again,
                    When manhood comes.

Fast speeds the time; we enter manhood's years;
Our youthful, fairy dreams so bright have fled,
And instead, the true and real aim of life.
Each castle once so grand, has been layed low
                    By wisdom's hand.

And wisdom now gives unto each his work,
While we begin our onward march to plan.
Fast we speed; till into the shadow of the wrong
We gaze; pressing on, still farther on,
                    We enter in

Unto the dark deceit of human strife
We startle at the sound, our ears are pained, our eyes
Seem not our own, yet, as we still go on,
It grows into a form a real shape of strife,
                    And wrong.

And we must now believe that all is true
Which we had thought a vague, uncertain sound.
We turn away almost bereft of sense,
To think this life contains so much
     Of wrong.

A wish steals in, an earnest wish. It is
That we might tear this chapter from life's book,
To place instead, a pleasant dream of youth.
It cannot be, the wish is vain, for time
Has led us down life's way, a score of years
     And ten.

We mark the time and distance well, unto the goal
Toward which we yet must strive; we feel a weight
Of strange perplexity and care; we see
A burden just before, which cannot well
     Be passed.

As we move on, the burden to us cleaves,
We lift it now, and it becomes a part
Of our own self. We look again; far down
The road of time, along the way, we see
     The throng.

And every one who travels on before,
Has his own burden tied, and well secured.
Another lesson learned on life's broad way,

'Tis now we see with mind and eyes made clear.
                    Experience

Has taught her lessons well.   Much less our burden
Seems, since learning this truth to tell   *   *
That for every heart that beats by the way,   *   *
There's a burden of grief for each.   The   *   *
                    Bubbled dreams.

Gold tinted rainbow hues.   The crystal balls
Have burst, each one.   The landscape now is earth's
Broad space.   We know the secrets of its face,
And farther on, there stands the dim, mysterious
                    Beyond.

Turning to God's mighty word, this truth we read,
That when life's school is done, our place in Para-
          dise
Must be just such an one as better fits
And well becomes our place and standing here.
                    God's truth.

We cannot enter through the gate until
We lay our lessons and our burdens down; if then
We've learned our lessons well in life's great school,
And stand approved of God, our light will shine
                    Through endless years.

And low before the throng we'll bend to praise,
And we will sing forever, glorious anthems
To our King.   No night is there, no wrong,
For God will sit upon the throne to make it all
One bright, eternal day; a pure, a peaceful
                              Holy rest.

John Moneybags.

———

John Moneybags sat in his easy chair,
Sleepily guileless of sorrow or care;
A thinking the thoughts which come sometimes,
And, oddly enough, shaped themselves into rhymes.
The glabrous expanse of his shiney pate
Reflected the glow of the fire, in the grate,
As he rubbed his fat hands then smoothed down his chin,
And looked 'round the room with a satisfied grin.

The room was tricked out with a Brummagin glare,
With a garnish of tinsel and upholstery, rare;
Windows, curtained, with a grand bizarre air,
The blinds but half closed, that the folks in the street,
Might see the room's toilet, clear down to its feet;—
As he faced his surroundings and thought of his pelf,—
Then opened the blinds wide,—careless like,—yet by
      stealth.

And his mind, retrospectively, wandered away
To the hills, where the home of his early youth lay.
'Twas the night of New Years day, and outside, the raw
And chilly air rasped like the teeth of a saw,
As it whistled through crevice of window and door.

13

And John was   *   *   *   *   Why bless me! just hear
    that man snore!

The gates of the past, have swung open before him,
The blue arch of youth's sunny sky now hangs o'er him,
And he sees with new rapture its purple and gold,
While beneath a broad elm, stands the cottage of old,
Where Bruno, the dog, still sleeps soundly before,
And the same leathern latch string hangs out at the door.

With the murmuring breeze, mingles odor of pine,
And the bleating of sheep and the lowing of kine,
With the clarion of cheer, from old Chanticleer's throat,
*And the chirrupy sound of the Chicadee's note.

The well-sweep, still casts its lean shadow before
The wood pile and chip-littered yard, near the door;
While the plough-boy, was following the oxen afield
With a vigor which only such labor can yield.

John crossed the old foot-bridge and mounting the stile,
He mused on each pleasant remembrance awhile;
Then, through the low gate-way, in one moment more,
He pulled at the latch-string, and opened the door.

When o'er his rapt senses a heavenly light
Like a vision of loveliness, broke on his sight;
Such a face and a form, as suggestively brings
The soul of a man, near the flutter of wings.

"Oh Mary!" —"oh John!" were the words which broke
      forth
With the first hearty, quick, respiration of both.
Then followed the history of years that were fled,
Retrospectively viewed as no better than dead.
Years hopelessly lost, years which none can recover
Be ye foolish or wise, be ye sweetheart or lover.

Then forth to the meadows with sauntering walk,
They spent the sweet moments, in social small talk,
Till the sun in the west, with an ominous frown,
Glared angrily, through the cloud's deepening brown.

A chilly wind, blew from the north
In fury fierce, with deafening roar,
The trembling forest bowed before
The blast, which swept in wreck and wrath,
While glowering blackness, drenched in gathering gloom
The path, the tempest strewed with sudden doom.

A calm succeeded;—over all
A sudden silence like a spell,
And thickening shadows black as hell
The earth enshrouded like a pall,—
And nature like a great, grim monster; saw
The Supreme God; and crouched in trembling awe.

John Moneybags fled, like a hunted hind,
And selfishly, left his dear Mary behind,

Nor stayed he to look to left or right
But ran to the foot-bridge with all his might.

When just half way over, the treacherous plank
Broke down, with his weight, like a plummet, he sank
Head first into the stream; choking, strangling, he grasped
At the plank,—which went floating down stream, while
      he gasped
And blowed like a porpoise, and shouting with terror--
He awoke; with the first hurried glance in the mirror,
He saw himself dripping, and limp as a rag,
And Andy, the servant, (a bit of a wag)
With a pitcher quite empty; and cocking his head,—
"You was wriggling just like an eel, on a spit
I thought you well nigh gone, in a fit."

John straightened himself ,glanced again in the glass
And said: "Never mind Andy, let it all pass;
Too much turkey and pudding I think, and for one,
I'm right glad New Years' day is over and gone."

Sad · Fate · of · Dogs.

Matter! matter! What's the clatter.
Tell me, tell me, what's the matter?
See the people running there,
What is broken, to repair?
Look! all are going, on the run;
Let's go too, and see the fun.

Well, here we are, and don't you see
It's not so great a mystery,
A pile of dogs! black, tan and white,
Ha! ha! it is a pleasant sight,
The city Fathers,—where are they?
All their commands we will obey,
For they are wise and frugal too,
They know just when to make ado.

But see! the dogs are coming in,
Those two indeed, look very thin.
A voice from out the waiting crowd,
It speaks in accents, clear and loud.
"Just pile them up, ten cubits high!
'Tis well that every dog should die."

The Mayor's voice, I do believe—
Or else I'm very much deceived.
The Mayor is a jolly man,
And for the town does all he can,
The Marshal too, looks well ahead,
And thinks 'tis best, the dogs are dead.
Indeed, they can no more bark
At ladies' horses on the Park;
It's many horses that have shied
From bark of dogs, quite hollow eyed,
And often, too, a runaway
Caused by those dogs that lifeless lay
Upon this pile of varied hue,
And then—O dear!! how much ado.

The other day, a lady said
Ten dogs were romping in her shed.
And every day, quite late in spring,
It was a very common thing
To see a well grown chicken dead!
But dogs must eat, and will be fed,
If owners have not half enough,
The dogs well know, 'tis very rough.

And soon they learn the art of stealing,
Doing all their desperate thieving,
When'er their hungry stomachs long;

Sometimes 'tis night, sometimes 'tis morn,
Indeed, it matters not what hour
For hunger gives them desperate power.

One day a lady on the square,
Carefully hung a nice fat pair
Of chickens, on two wooden pegs;
Hung them quite secure, by the legs.
That night she woke; she heard a sound
Robbers! sure! -The husband slept profound.
She punched him; then a double punch
He woke to say, "You are a dunce.
'Tis nothing sure, but dogs or cats
Or, very likely, 'tis the rats."

"Ah, no!" she softly, softly said,
I heard them talking in the shed,
And just before, along the walk,
I heard two tread and softly talk;
I'm sure I heard a whistle low,
And then I heard a thumping slow
Oh dear! you will be shot—O dear!
Don't go without your gun—O dear!"

The husband went in search of game;
He said, "I'll take the surest aim."
The wife could not control her fear;
She thought a dozen robbers near,—

Then came a quick and loud report,
She feared the robbers held the fort.
Rushing in haste upon the scene,
To shield her husband from the fiend,
It seemed to her a frantic dream.

She thought her husband pale through fear
And yet, no robbers were seen near.
The husband spake and said, "My dear,
That robber ne'er will come again
For turkey, chicken, meat or hen;
There lies his body, look and see,
Ha! ha! he's dead, as dead can be.

"When I came out, I counted four,
But all the rest flew through the door
And my quick aim just hit the last
As he was nearly half way past.
But see! your chickens lay all ways,
The dogs well know the house that pays,
The ice chest door stands open wide,
All the food is dragged outside."

Well, well, that pile has much increased,
And we must now our stories cease.
To the Mayor our thanks are due—
And all the "City Fathers" too,
For they have really done their best,

To send these dogs to peaceful rest.
'Tis better far, than living in town,
Roaming the streets, at night and morn
Stealing the chickens, that never do more
Than scratch for a living, round the barn door.

MORAL.

Now give your dogs, my boys, enough to eat
Of bread that's stale, or something hashed with
    meat,
If once a day they eat a good square meal,
They'll be content and will not care to steal.

Hulda Kukowski.

Houstie Goutie was a thriving town,
And in that town lived Martin Brown.

He married when quite old in life,
Hulda Kukowski, a girlish wife.

The people thought it a strange marriage;
They lived in style and owned a carriage.

Three children came to give them joy,
Two girls, and last of all a boy.

But death crept in and brought them pain,
God took these to himself again.

This sorrow turned poor Hulda's mind
From worldly cares to prose and rhyme.

She thought and wrote, and wrote and thought,
And this to her much comfort brought.

Unfortunate! indeed, her husband's head
Could not on prose and rhymes be fed.

It oft had made him quite enraged,
When he found Hulda thus engaged.

In writing to her friends a line,
He said, "'Twas all a waste of time."
Nor did he once suspect the rhyme.

By chance, he had a hint one day,
Which opened up a little ray

Of light upon an unknown page,
And then he flew into a rage

Which lasted till he went to tea,
When he seemed vexed as man could be.

Poor Hulda could not even guess
What made her husband strangely press

The subject worn of "Woman's Rights,"
He talked so loud of woman's flights

On Pegasus, in lofty style,
And other foolish dames beguile.

He said, "They'd better knead more bread,
Then let such subjects turn their head."

Hulda trembled, every inch,
But thought it not quite best to flinch.

And yet, from this time on she knew
Her hours for writing would be few.

And every day she stood in fear
That he would secretly draw near

And find her well arranged effusions,
Which he would say were but delusions.

She stood in fear of uncle Marth,
In fear of his unbounded wrath

In case he found her—O! how shocking—
A well-established, true, "Blue Stocking."

But fate, which turns all things in time,
Turned Hulda's thoughts away from rhyme.

Her health gave out; the doctor said
"On different food she must be fed.

A change of air might do her good,"
And this her friends all understood.

She took the change, and thousands gave
To foreign climes her health to save.

But all her travels far and near,
And every comfort bought so dear

Seemed not to give the boon she sought,
For unto her no good it wrought.

And when she to her home returned,
Her friends professed that they discerned.

A change that no one dare deny,
Aunt Hulda soon must surely die.

At last she shunned all medical advice,
Well knowing that, at any price,

Could not restore her wasted frame;
She said, "My life's a fading flame.

It cannot, cannot be restored;
This truth it must not be deplored."

When Springtime came she suffered pain
That seemed to well consume her brain.

'Twas then the doctor gently said,
"On no more food she should be fed,

But let the friends do all that's best
To give her nerves much quiet rest."

For days they watched with tender care,
And only whispered words they dare.

One morn she called them to her bed,
And soon they wept, for she was dead.

In quite good time they found her rhyme,
The husband said, "It was sublime."

He also said, "I think it strange,
That Hulda could all this arrange

Without my knowledge, care and praise."
Indeed, if I had known her ways,

I would have helped her anxious brain,
And she would then, have won much fame.

"'Tis strange this secret she should keep,
And not my help and wisdom seek."

He seemed to suffer much remorse,
Because at times he had been cross.

He never dreamed that Hulda's mind
Was on such lofty heights inclined.

He praised and praised, as on he read,
Alas, Aunt Hulda then—was dead.

Domestic Economy in Tantrumdaygo Territory, 1801.

Sally Grum and Henry Flarr,
A newly wedded cautious pair,
Discussed the matter well one day,
Regarding ways and means that pay.
The husband bent on frugal ways,
Was really hurt and quite amazed,
When his dear bride in accents firm,
Said, "Now I was eldest born
A family of six with ne'er a son,
And ever since I straight could walk,
I've been most carefully well taught,
The mysteries of household work."

I've heard this sound both night and day,
By your mother you must stay;
Bring some wood in, watch the fire,
Wash the face of little Ryer;
Rock the baby to its sleep;
Make the house look clean and neat;
Spread the table, sweep the floor,
Drive the flies from out the door—

Sometimes, 'twould take no little grit,
To give the anger no permit.
Indeed, I answered every call,
And did my duty well, for all.
I've helped my father count the cost,
Of all the dollars spent or lost;
And now 'tis time I think, my dear,
For me to rest from anxious fear.
I ne'er shall see a better chance,
To run and visit, play and dance.

Now I suggest a boarding place,
In a small family of taste.
Then I can have a rest quite rare,
From all this work, and household care.
By other hands 'twill then be done;
And, still again, I'm very sure
That we can use their furniture.
And too, if I'm not well deceived,
We'll all our company receive
Into their parlor neat and warm.
We need not rise at early dawn.
We'll have no care of buying, buying;
In rainy days no clothes a drying.

No sweeping cobwebs, blacking stoves;
No baking pies or pounding cloves.
No waiting on the door for all

The numerous friends that then will call.
Indeed, from all these cares relieved,
Which often has my spirit grieved.
And listen dear to what I say,
For this hard work we will not pay,
I think much more than half the cost
Of hiring house, and your time lost
In nailing carpets, bringing wood,
And helping, helping as you should,
To carry water for the cooking,
And after all the groceries looking.
And then—'twould be a horrid bore
For you to help me scrub the floor.

Now Henry dear; think on these cares;
And don't believe that these are airs
Put on just now, because I'm married;
Don't say at heart, I wish I'd tarried
From these domestic, trying troubles,
If marrying, cares like these it doubles.

The husband thought on all she said.
Could not deny, he felt some dread.
He turned the matter in his mind;
To all these truths he had been blind.
He pondered well for several days,
Then gave his wife some heartfelt praise.
He had counted every inch anew,

And found her words were then quite true;
For, at the estimates he had run,
'Twould cost, he said, three times the sum
To open up a house complete;
And furnished simply, only neat.
Then, interest on the money paid,
To say no words about a maid
To do the horrid kitchen work.

Then to his wife he softly said;
My dear, there's wisdom in your darling head.
I now believe to save the clatter
Of all this buying, buying, buying,
And our brains on cares applying,
We'll try it, just one year to board,
And the surplus of our money to hoard.

A lady, just the one, was found,
Who, loath at first, said, "there is room;
Come to my house, I'll take you soon,
And try at least to do my best,
And in my parlor you may rest.
The room above is very neat;
Indeed, both rooms are quite complete.
The chamber eighteen feet and square;
Is large enough for any pair.
The bedstead with a hair mattress,
A carpet fine, of colors fast,

The windows, two, are hung with lace.
The parlor is a quiet place;
Where my piano just now stands;
And 'tis not used by many hands.
For all these privileges so rare,
Believing you a quiet pair,
I'll give these rooms just as you see,
And ask the sum of four times three.
Twelve dollars every week for two,
And this is cheap, because 'tis you."
The couple reasoned very fast,
And much before a day had passed,
They settled in their crafty minds,
That this was just the lucky chance.

When well disposed of in this home,
For gold to save their hearts did long.
In counting up the hours and days,
They found themselves in quite a haze.
If they had planned by month to settle
They would then saved have quite a little.
Astonishing indeed! in dollars six.
This fact, it seemed a dreadful fix,
But what to do, they did not know,
As month on month began to grow.

The wife one day caught some idea.
"O Hub!" she said, "away with fear;

We will be sharp and not complain;
But let us ask this quiet dame,
If she would very much object,
To take her pay for board and rooms,
In larger sums, say every month;
As often as your salary comes."

The dame, not thinking any wrong
Would come from this new artful song,
Said, "It's one, and all the same to me;
And to accommodate, I now agree
To take my pay in larger sums,
As often as your salary comes.
To me, 'tis well, and all the same;"
So spake the kind and quiet dame.
Alas, alas, she had not thought
While glad and anxious to accommodate,
That this request was just a bate,
From out her purse to catch some gain;
And thus to her, 'twas all the same.

Now when the next pay did appear,
She thought, and thought it very queer,
That such a check to her did come;
And to her almanac, quick she run.
She found herself outwitted, sure,
The extra days just counted four.

And then, in counting two months time,
The extra days she found were nine.

She said no words till next month came.
Well had she planned; (as woman can)
To rid herself of such a knave,
Who unto her much trouble gave.
When next he paid his scanty dues,
She said, I'll give you now, some honest truths:
You've had your time to settle as you please;
I think your mind must be diseased,
Or else you take me for a fool complete,
That in this way you try to cheat.
I took you in against my will;
Of anxious care I've had my fill;
An extra girl I've had to hire,
To tend the door, and watch your fire;
And have I not, how many times
Prepared for you an extra lunch;
'Tis now I see I was a dunce.
Just think! for all this work and care,
And common use of silver plate,
You choose to cheat me of my rate.
You both may deem this high-toned fun,
But I am ready now to dun.
Just give me what you honest owe,
And then pack up your duds and go.

Hunt for yourselves a house to keep;
'Tis then you'll find you cannot cheat.
You oft will count your days ahead;
But still in counting, counting fine,
I know you will not miss the nine.

You thought perhaps I would not mind,
Because I used you well and kind.
But business, business is, when straight;
I'll not be cheated of my rate.
I'm well inclined, and have a heart
Which oft is touched by mercy's dart.
These long, long months, I've worked and planned,
While cares increased on every hand.
I'll give you now just seven days,
To find a place that's to your taste.
Then we, without regret will part,
And you must try to cleanse your heart.
Don't think that when I say good bye,
To board another I shall try.

Mistakes.

'Tis said that every soul comes into life
Under the influence of some peculiar star.
If this be true, then all our acts are fixed,
Or held in bondage by that far off star.
And if the course it marks be full of ill,
No matter how we run, or what we will,
We'll meet no other fate but constant wrong;
And what we say, or what may be our song,
Mistakes will meet us sure on every turn.
And let our conscience be as heaven's snow flakes
The whiteness soon, will be a harvest of mistakes.

I thought there was a star, who's twinkling laugh
Would never fail to light my joyous path.
And yet, since youth, that star has changed my life,
Shedding a certain gloom, my joy to blight.
It oft has sent confusion to my thought
When all my motives well and true, were wrought,
No difference what the work of plans have been,
If I seem bent on something right to win,
Long enough before the work is done,
Some dark mistake is sure to come.

Mistakes, mistakes, until I see 'tis plain
That all my life, that star will never wane.
But what care I, so long as God will hear
And answer this request, which I hold dear,
That he will lift the scales from my blind eyes,
And 1 may clearly see my way, to Paradise.

Gossips.

TO A. B.

In these thy careless, youthful sunny days,
'Tis well to learn some valuable truths.
Which never can be culled from books, alone.
Thousands gather up these truths in ways
Which have been vexed and sore, in rugged paths
Their feet were torn upon the rough-edged rocks
Briers held them sometimes, fast, and then
The grip of patience loosed its hold and grief,
Came in to swell the flood of anguish into tears.
One strays into these ways quite unaware,
For often they seem wonderfully fair.
But you, dear friend, must learn this very day
How to evade the roughness of these briery snares.
Reject with scorn the idle flatterers story.
Reject the one who mars the face of truth
With words so sweet and plausable— yet wrong.
Reject the one who brings to you a story
Made up of Madam Gossip's odds and ends
And asks that you would give a mild accent
Or, just as he would choose to put his words
You cannot well escape the natural no;

But with your answer, be it yes, or no,
He'll then, to other gossips hurrying go
To represent in bright and glowing terms
That you! alas, have filled their cup with woe.

Index.

www.ingramcontent.com/pod-product-compliance
Lightning Source LLC
Chambersburg PA
CBHW030624270326
41927CB00007B/1296